Alice McVeigh was b[...]
diplomatic family, an[...]
13, when her family r[...]
to play the cello, [...]
Washington Young C[...] .....ard and the Beethoven
Society of Washington cello competition, as well as being a
national finalist in the National Music Teachers Association
Young Soloists competition. She achieved a BMus with
distinction in performance at Indiana University in 1980, and
later that year came to London to study privately with
William Pleeth. Since then she has freelanced with orchestras
including the BBC Symphony Orchestra, the Royal
Philharmonic Orchestra and Sir John Eliot Gardiner's
Orchestre Révolutionnaire et Romantique throughout the
UK, the EU, America and the Far East. Her two novels
(*While the Music Lasts* and *Ghost Music*) were published by
Orion in the late 1990s, and her first play (*Beating Time*) will
be published in 2003 by New Theatre Productions. She has
just finished her third novel, *Remember me*. Her husband
Simon is Professor of Music at Goldsmiths College,
University of London; they have a five-year-old daughter,
Rachel.

Noel Ford, who has been a contributor to *Punch* and *Private
Eye* for many years, is currently editorial cartoonist for eight
national publications. In a previous existence he was once
lead guitarist with a rock (later dinner-dance) band. After one
corporate gig too many, he decided to hang up his Gibson
and concentrate his efforts on the much more secure
profession of freelance cartoonist. He recently emigrated to
Wales from where he draws cartoons for clients all around the
world in a studio complete with computers, guitars and a
digital piano. As Dog Cartoonist of the Year, he once, to his
everlasting shame, posed for a national newspaper outside the
Café Royale with a Bonio dog biscuit clamped between his
teeth.

Also by Alice McVeigh

While the Music Lasts

(Orion hardback, 1994;
Phoenix paperback, 1995)

Ghost Music

(Orion hardback, 1997;
Oriel paperback, 1998)

All Risks Musical

AN IRREVERENT GUIDE

to the music profession

Alice McVeigh

With cartoons by
Noel Ford

POCKET PRESS
CATERHAM • SURREY

All Risks Musical
an irreverent guide to the music profession

First published in Great Britain in 2002 by
POCKET PRESS
The Old Stables, 10 Timber Lane, Caterham, Surrey CR3 6LZ

A CIP catalogue record for this book is available from
the British Library.

ISBN 0-9544040-0-9

Noel Ford's work is sourced through www. CartoonStock.com

All Risks Musical, www.allrisksmusical.com

Cover and book design by Cecil Smith

Typeset in Galliard by
EVERGREEN GRAPHICS
11 The Drive, Craigweil on Sea, Aldwick, West Sussex PO21 4DU

Printed and bound in Great Britain by
ANTONY ROWE LIMITED
Bumper's Farm, Chippenham, Wiltshire SN14 6LH

For
Sviatoslav Prokofiev
who always understands

It was the morning after the concert before. Eyes still blurry with sleep, I inspected the post, which included an insurance form for the most recent addition to my cello stable.

This instrument is hereby insured for ALL RISKS MUSICAL

it informed to whom it might concern, i.e. me.

The longer I looked at that phrase, the longer something in that notion appealed to me. I wished that I had been lucky enough to have been insured against all such risks before charging down the path of professional cello-playing. I wished that Someone Who Knew had slipped me the truth about orchestras before I'd made all the mistakes I'd made over the past ten or twelve years. I sat down at my word-processor waiting, as musicians do, for the phone to ring. It didn't, as it happened, and two days later this slim volume was history.

Future biographers will note, and dissertation students surmise, that it just spilled out. Too right it did. I have written, since the age of eight, some really dire poetry, more plays than I care to recall, a turgidly adolescent romance and about seven novels, none of which cost me long hours of insomnia. I am not one of those writers who, upon sighting an empty screen, start gibbering and pulling their hair out in clumps. I like empty screens. Compared to conductors, they are harmless. Compared to rabid cello principals, thoughtless fixers and bows in chronic need of a rehair, they are manageable. Writing, like cello-playing, is a breeze, as long as you are not attempting to do it for a living.

Some UK music students have already imbibed these rules in various lectures, but I am not so modest as to have written for would-be orchestral hacks alone. What is contained in these rules is a microcosm of human nature, human nature writ small. We all know players less gifted than ourselves who seem to do better than we do — as well as near-geniuses who succeed rather less well. If various things about the profession have always puzzled you, the answers are probably here, in this handy little volume. Buy a few for your friends; tell your rivals it's rotten. Slip it in your aspiring kiddie's Christmas stocking. Here it is: human nature laid bare. Welcome to the unwritten rules. Welcome to the truth about orchestras.

RULE 1: You have never heard the joke that your principal, for reasons best known to himself, wants to tell you. Nor have you ever heard a funnier. Remember, the reason best known to himself may be to determine whether you have a sense of humour.

*You have never heard the joke
that your principal wants to tell you.*

RULE 2: The orchestra you most enjoy playing with is … the one you are presently engaged by, regardless of any genuine preference. If you can't think of one amazing principal player, one half-decent conductor, or any remotely plausible reason for this opinion, then remember, it's really all down to the *people*, isn't it.

*The orchestra you most enjoy playing with
is the one you are presently engaged by.*

RULE 3: Conductors, almost without exception, are rubbish. This is a given, and only partly because it is (all too often) true. You must never admit to admiring a conductor, or enjoying his concert, unless you are currently stuck on a broken-down tube train with the carver in question.

The rule for soloists is more complicated. If they treat the orchestra like a group of fellow human beings, and do not happen to play the same instrument as you, you may approve. If they do play the same instrument as you, they are instead insanely lucky, slept with the entire Tchaikovsky Competition panel, rode their family connections for all they were worth, etc.

RULE 4: Whenever possible, take care to compliment principals of all sections on well-played solos. They are, to a principal, neurotic about their performances and receive precious few plaudits from the regulars. This has the advantage of securing your reputation as a discerning judge of true musicality. (If you can manage to diplomatically trash principals from rival orchestras at the same time, so much the better.)

Take care to compliment your principals.

RULE 5: Cultivate the art of being a good listener. Allow the sweet but dull soul at the back of the seconds to describe his prize-winning roses, or the piccolo player his practically pornographic photography. These are the people who, during your absences, will remind the fixer to ask you back. It is also worth remembering that power in orchestras is not always concentrated where you might expect. There are people of prime influence at the back of nearly every section, as well as principals thoroughly out of favour with the majority. Because of the unlikelihood of your sorting all this out first time in, follow this simple rule: If in doubt, fascinate.

Be a good listener.

*Never fail to appear to be
having a good time.*

RULE 6: Be memorable. Don't slink in, do the job, and slink out. It may be theoretically possible to build a freelance career without being friendly, good-natured and extrovert, but in practice it rarely happens. Be open, be chatty, buy any number of drinks, and never fail to appear (despite quietly loathing it) to be having a good time. It is strange but true that regular players, however crusty or cynical they may appear, prefer to be surrounded by cheerful faces. The fact that most of their own faces are suicidal may have something to do with this.

RULE 7: Never complain, even when everyone around you is complaining. Smile, but resist the impulse to agree that (a) you've never played in a group with such slipshod organisation, (b) the temperature in the hall is several degrees below zero, or (c) the entire management of the tour should be shot. Such remarks, in common with most remarks, tend to get around, and while orchestra members are expected and sometimes even encouraged to complain, it can be work-death for an extra to string along.

RULE 8: Dress decently, that is, slightly above the average. This suggests, however erroneously, that you are a professional with pride in your work, and has the additional merit of exhibiting your best features to advantage. No one in the orchestra will notice, but, strangely enough, the management is likely to, having an inbuilt bias towards style over substance. Your concert clothes in particular should be above reproach, particularly in their general condition. The only exception to this rule must be obvious: try not to flaunt any financial triumph where it might prove galling to the orchestra in which you are guesting. This is especially true when playing with regional orchestra players, who despise and envy Londoners about equally. Figure out when to leave that divinely expensive little black dress at home.

A similar rule applies to hitting the right balance when asked, as one inevitably is, how work is in London. Remember that practically every regional player is secretly dying to try his luck there, and tailor your answer accordingly. Don't be afraid to admit it when times are hard; a modest sufficiency is the mark to aim at. Oddly enough, this will not sink you in the estimation of your listeners, unless of course you never manage to work anywhere. They will be altogether more suspicious of the player who charges around Dyfed bragging about their *Harry Potter* film sessions, and who's to say they're not right?

RULE 9: Speaking of being right, your principal is always right, particularly when she is so hopelessly wrong that open discussion of her shortcomings prevails. If she chooses to put up-bows over fortissimo chords, then that's just the way you like to bow chords yourself. (When you're the principal, of course, it's your chance to ride over the objections of hapless pedestrians and traffic.)

RULE 10: (String players only) Get the bowings in. I admit that, as long as your technique is sufficiently sharp, it makes very little difference to the product. But tell that to the cross old lady in the tenth row, who thinks it looks sloppy, and tell that to the eagle-eyed fixer looking for an excuse to replace you with someone more generally malleable. If you can't get the bowings in during the rehearsal, or if you're sitting behind a principal sadistically intent upon altering everything, it is occasionally acceptable to be observed copying bowings during a rehearsal break. But don't make a habit of this, as it has an uncanny look of being teacher's pet about it. Being teacher's pet may of course get you 'in' with the principal: but, sooner or later, even he may unfairly assume that, since you always take so much trouble, you can't really be all that good. (Nobody knows why this is.)

RULE 11: Do not practise. Yes, yes, I know as well as you do that you 'didn't get where you are today' without practising ferociously for at least one decade of your life. But don't do it before the concert, in the middle of the rehearsal, or during a break. The simple reason for this idiotic rule is that British orchestras are the best sight-readers in the world. British players can sight-read anything: this is the foundation of every orchestra schedule in the country. Naturally enough, it isn't true, but it is not your responsibility to make this obvious. Your job is to keep a stiff upper lip and get on with it. To be brutal: your duty is to fake. The British are the best fakers in the world.

And think about it. What are the odds against your fixer/conductor/principal hearing you massacring the famous Storm from Beethoven's 'Pastoral' and thinking, 'At last! The sound I have been looking for all my life!' And what, frankly, are the odds against these same people thinking, 'So *that*'s the nerd with the reedy tone whose intonation has been driving me quietly bonkers all morning?' Even if it wasn't you, the desire to blame is there. Don't give anybody ammunition. Keep your head down and charge out of the trenches, rifle loaded, grenade at the ready. Ready, aim, FAKE!

RULE 12: Don't stick orchestra stickers on your instrument case, or fatuous slogans either. The orchestra you guest with today is the one that rubs you out tomorrow; and the less obvious *that*'s made, the better. Let your case be the black, mysterious one, giving nothing away. You might have just popped in from the LSO or alternatively from your temp. job, but no one should be able to guess which from your case. (They may of course get some idea from your playing, but you can't win them all.)

RULE 13: Take care whom you're speaking to. Just the other day I heard about a player who, as the orchestra was asked to re-tune for the tenth time by a pernickety oboe principal, turned to his desk-partner and groaned, 'Oh God, I've heard about him!' Which might not have mattered had not the desk-partner been the oboist's wife, as well as a fixer in her own right. I was myself rubbed out of one eminent orchestra after complaining of a slow and torturous brain-death in the hearing of the conductor, who had (God knows why) thought comparatively highly of his effort... So be vigilant and watchful. Today's mere desk-partner could be the principal cellist's mistress tomorrow; indeed, if the principal cellist runs true to form, this may even be the case today. And guess who was in the loo cubicle while you were trashing the Beeb's latest squeaky-door offering? (Answer: the fixer's girlfriend.)

RULE 14: Neither over-booze nor under-booze. It may seem hilarious to be obliged to warn people in any profession against not drinking enough, but in orchestras it can still happen. If massive boozing is the norm in the band (or, more likely, section of the band) in which you find yourself, prepare to massively booze during your free time. It's either that or a doctor's certificate, and even that may not square you with the principal trumpet, unless sufficiently oiled. Drinking is a fact of orchestral life, even though in some circles it is quietly falling from fashion.

It can obviously be damaging to over-booze and perform, but a handful of our finest orchestra players are brilliant enough to get away with it. Assuming you're not one of these, you'll have to draw the line, once you get established enough to say no, unless of course you prefer to find yourself washed up at fifty, with your liver, your home life and your career shot to pieces.

Neither over-booze nor under-booze.

RULE 15: Keep your musical, religious, and political opinions to yourself. You may imagine that your conductor will be riveted by your exposition of how marvellous Sir Simon Rattle was in this passage: curiously enough, he could not in fact be less interested (unless of course, he *is* Sir Simon Rattle, in which case you might expect the most flattering attention). Alternatively, you might consider it crucial that you pass on your message of personal salvation as a Scientologist, a Jehovah's Witness or a member of the Animal Liberation Front. Fine. Do. But pass it on outside working hours, amongst strangers, and preferably while heavily false-moustached. You might feel so strongly about some political issue (fox-hunting, leader-baiting) that you feel everyone of even moderate common sense is bound to agree with you. Unfortunately this may not stop them from disagreeing — or even complaining to the fixer about 'the noisy oik at the back of the seconds'.

The corollary of this rule is that, even if some-one attacks your gender, race, sexual preferences, or most deeply-held beliefs, you are obliged to smile and politely change the subject. Someone in the full-time orchestra, that is, or in management. You are at perfect liberty to take exception to insults from your fellow freelances at your own discretion, making due allowance for the possibility that time and/or the oddities of the profession may one day make a bleeding principal out of them.

RULE 16: Flirtation is mandatory. Of course it is. It is in life, so why exempt freelancing? Your husband's boss requires reassurance that, at 75, he is still a sex symbol, so why shouldn't the sub-principal double bass? Since most of the powerful positions in orchestras continue to be held by men (except, crucially, in the authentic-instrument world) this attitude still comes with the territory. Despite amazing advances in recent years, women players can still expect to be teased, caressed, not taken seriously and even (though rarely) insulted. Fellow females, I urge you to recognise that this is Life. These men imagine they're brightening up your day: let them. The harm it does to you is minimal; and most of them are really too old-fashioned to learn. Besides, time is on our side. The number of women being professionally trained greatly exceeds the number of men — as it has for some years. There is even a theory that, at some point, men may wind up being the endangered species in Britain's top orchestras. I can't quite imagine it personally, but that doesn't mean it won't happen.

RULE 17: Cheer up the poor sods. Those of us looking enviously at the blissful certainties of

those in full-time orchestra work tend to forget —
God knows why, as orchestra members make it
blindingly obvious — that members of full-time
groups are, almost by definition, bitterly unhappy.
As we sit at home waiting for the diary service to
ring, it seldom occurs to us to pity the poor
bastards rushing from one session to another.
Thinking of the difference between their bank
balances and ours seems — oddly enough — to
make pity impossible. But the truth is, they're
nearly all miserable. They've forgotten the middle
name of their youngest; they're living from one
beta-blocker to the next; their liver's making
indisputable noises of complaint; they've been on
four tours too many this year; and that one-night-
stand in Amsterdam has made them nervy about
AIDS. They are, in short, a mess. They need
cheerful faces around them; that is, faces other
than their own.

How can you improve their spirits? By recalling
what your mother used to tell you about how
there are always people worse off than you.
Reminding overworked orchestra A that orchestra
B is not only equally dead-on-its-feet but very
nearly bankrupt can do wonders for team morale.
Players in every orchestra are always convinced —
in the teeth of all the evidence — that theirs is the
only orchestra with too much or not enough
work, the highest ratio of unbearable to bearable

conductors, and so on. Nobody, these days, needs reminding that orchestral times are hard, only that they could be even worse. It's live and let die out there in the musical jungle. So get out and swing from tree to tree, while there are still a few trees left standing.

RULE 18: Aim for the last chair. This may seem a perfectly obvious recommendation, in that it is infinitely more agreeable to be promoted than rebuffed, but an amazing number of young musicians don't seem to realise it. Their first move, on a freelance date, seems to be to see how far forward they can wiggle without someone blowing the whistle on them. The fault lies partly with fixers, who never seem to understand that seating order matters, indeed rankles, more than anything else (except money, of course). Their light suggestion, 'Oh, sit where you like, except for Geoff, who's leading,' can lead to all kinds of ill feeling, almost as much as their putting little Evangeline, who's never done the 'Eroica' before, in front of Jed, who's done it all, including time. It takes stunning diplomacy not to alienate Jed, twice your age and nearly twice your size, after a careless fixer has slotted you in ahead of him. The way to play it is like this: 'I think Mac must have been plastered when he was doing the seating. If you see me about to come in wrong, can you clue me in?' This will probably not deceive Jed, but may still mollify him.

Seating order matters.

Non-musicians may sneer, but seating matters to players. This is probably because, rightly or wrongly, the audience and even fellow players will interpret your distance away from the conductor as a commentary on your ability. As it is rare for people to resent being put behind their more experienced elders, I increasingly believe that, with the exception of the front desks, age should determine seating entirely. Indeed — strangely enough — I seem to see more intrinsic merit in this scheme with each passing year.

In the meantime, however, aim for the back. Let the fixer yelp, 'For Christ's sake, you're meant to be number two!' in front of everyone. Rather that than his sidling up to you at number two saying in some confusion, 'I'm terribly sorry, but you're on fourth desk today.' Such an embarrassing occurrence might preclude his ever wishing to see you again, wherever you sit. So, sit at the back with your chin held high. The ideal at which I aim is hordes of string players clambering over each other in their anxiety to reach that yearned-for last chair. It will never happen: our worries about other people's perceptions will never permit such a charming display of mass modesty. But aim for the back and see, in the long run, if it doesn't pay off. 'And the last shall be first.' Ring a bell, does it?

RULE 19: And while you're there, look as if you're at the back. Don't sway about like a seasick Du Pré, and don't bob up and down proposing bowings to your betters. Just sit down and shut up. Play powerfully, by all means; but don't poke out the eye of the nearest viola-player in the excess of your passion. That kind of approach is reserved, unofficially, for section leaders. Nobody, upon observing this behaviour, thinks, 'Good Lord, that fellow should be leading,' as you fondly imagine. People think instead, 'Who on earth is the prat at the back of the cellos?' They may even think it if you're at the front of the cellos, although that's slightly unfair, and a certain amount of show-biz is acceptable when leading. The whole idea is faintly un-British, however, and the lines, while invisible, are acutely drawn. If in doubt, don't sway about, sums it up. Nobody, you may be sure, will criticise you for not doing.

RULE 20: Support your freelance principal. Despite a lurking suspicion that you would have played an infinitely more subtle solo than Eloise, compliment her profusely after both rehearsal and concert. She is undoubtedly as aware as you of any deficiencies, and, were you to be less than loyal, might be pleased to blame your attitude for her lamentable performance. If you can manage not to entirely outplay Eloise, even to make the odd error, noticeable only by her, she will probably consider you an asset, and even recommend you to replace her the next time she's unavailable. Arrogantly outshine her, query her sillier bowings, or make suggestions to the conductor over her head, on the other hand, and you'll probably find yourself relieved of even your comparatively humble position. (You'd forgotten, hadn't you, that Eloise was at the Academy with the conductor's wife…)

RULE 21: Support your major orchestra principal. A tricky one, this, because these poor souls spend half their waking hours fielding adoring phone calls from would-be extras and being generally fawned upon. The other extras may even openly court them, attending their forgettable Wigmores, angling for social invitations, and so on. Sometimes it can be a refreshing change for at least one extra to just let a principal be. But this will only prove the case if you make it clear in subtle ways that you remain a paid-up member of the unofficial fan club. An especially warm smile from you following his little solo could be enough, though some leader's egos will demand the ritual compliment. However, no one is recommending you hang on your leader's lips, burbling about 'exquisite craftsmanship and tone', like a broadsheet review. This kind of behaviour might expose you to cruel jibes from other members and extras. Not to mention the danger that the shrewder type of principal might begin to think (a) you're not as secure about your playing as you ought to be, or even (b) 'I vant to be alone'.

RULE 22: Don't be an instrument bore. This is mainly a rule for string players, as the snobbery attached to a 1680 violin is quite different from the cachet attached to a modern trumpet. But it really is snobbery. Nobody cares whether your violin was made by Amati minor or by Bloggs of Scunthorpe as long as you made it through the frigging audition. If asked, especially during a mine-is-posher-than-yours routine, you may admit that your bow is one of Tourte's riper efforts, but otherwise just keep moving it across the strings. Let your colleagues suppose that the ethereal beauty of your sound is due to sheer skill alone. And don't get caught by the boy-did-I-ever-land-a-bargain game, either. You'd be amazed how less agreeable people will find you upon learning that your Gagliano was bought at a craft fayre for thirty quid. It is a regrettable fact of human nature that we find it hard to rejoice in someone's scoring over us, that jealousy seems to bar the route to affection. The person who comes out best in these little games is the one who admits, 'It's not a brilliant violin, but I'm saving up to buy a better one.'

Don't be an instrument bore.

RULE 23: Don't send in the clowns. As deputies, that is, or replacements for yourself. It may occasion gales of hollow laughter as I remind you that there are times when, obliged to play in two places at once, you may be requested to recommend another player in your stead. You will be tempted, as by Lucifer, to send in the most oafish professional of your acquaintance, so that the fixer, one of that famously fickle breed, can't use his advent as an excuse to replace you permanently. Turn your back on this temptation. Don't send the most scintillating player you know, but don't chance a dud either. Keep in mind all those solid-but-dull sorts that, naturally enough, get scarcely any work, and hand one of these the job. What is on trial here is your judgement. No fixer will thank you for making the performance less good than it might have been; and your seal of approval should be seen to rise above mediocrity — unless you enjoy having your musicality queried when you're not even on hand to defend yourself.

RULE 24: Auditions and trials. There is precious little that can be usefully said about auditions. If the panel is likely to be male, then sedately sexy is the line to take in dress. If the powers that be are female, then go for the unflinchingly professional look. (These rules are usually reversed for male applicants.) A business-like smile and the occasional handshake is all that is likely to be required of you socially, although the informal interview (usually consisting of that boring gambit: 'what is your instrument?') is sometimes tacked on at the end. Behave as naturally as you can manage, and don't forget to thank your pianist. Don't gabble, in your relief that you played well. Don't be drawn into whether or not you really want the job (if the audition is in fact for a job). Say thanks, and buzz off.

Trials, now, you could write a book about trials, which in truth include half the jobs you are engaged on. The traditional trial is, of course, a trial period spent holding down an orchestral job for which you, along with several others, are being seriously considered. However, given the nature of freelancing, I urge you to imagine yourself to be permanently on trial with one group or another. All the advice contained in this slim vol. is true of trials — I should perhaps add, even more true of trials.

Members of orchestras are fond of saying that jobs are awarded to those who best 'fit in'. This is obviously true up to a point (although the sceptic might well marvel: what price all those howling disaster-zones that are there already? were they

Pick up signals.

reckoned to fit in too?), but I would add this useful corollary: orchestra jobs go to those who get on the nerves of the fewest members. Not bugging people, in other words, is at least as crucial as getting on with them. Not being noisy or self-aggrandising, or feeble or cocksure or too-shy or any number of things — the whole differing bewilderingly from orchestra to orchestra, for the same violinist may be reckoned 'too quiet' for one orchestra and 'too chatty' for another. You will have to be electrically sensitive to ambience in order to figure out what kind of band you're involved with, and there is no sure guide. Even from section to section, what's wanted may be different, and it's almost certainly got nothing to do with your level of skill, because most principals will admit that most triallists would be excellent in most jobs. In fact, competition is now such that most *applicants* could at least manage to hold down most jobs.

So, assuming you've been offered a trial and none of those rare stupidities has occurred (where the job is offered to your rival before you even start your trial, and no, I'm not making it up), what can you do to improve your chances? Put out your antennae, that's what. Pick up signals. If the aged crustacean sitting beside you in the basses says, 'Oscar always moans we're too loud in this bit,' then shut the hell up. If the principal lightly remarks, 'Personally, I like my Debussy with a lot of welly,' then don't spare the horses, or the rosin either. If you notice that the principal, for reasons best known to his osteopath, plays spiccato at the point, then that is the precise place where your spiccato works best. And if anybody asks you whether you really want the job, you really really do — whatever the truth might be. It is extraordinarily insulting to an orchestra to hear from some young upstart that he's actually hoping to be offered a higher position in a rival orchestra, whether or not his hope might be based in reality. And it is galling for an orchestra to waste time and money trialling people who seek nothing more than their name on his c.v.

Once you've been offered the job is the time to give your reasons, with deepest regret, for declining the great honour, and even then, you need a bloody good excuse. A death in the family, preferably yours, is the best excuse, followed by a surprise appointment in government. The offer of a better-paying job will do, though there will be some discontent, whereas the likely real reason (that you may be fed up freelancing but you'd be even more fed up working full-time, and anyway your entire goal was clambering onto the extra list) is completely unacceptable. (If you happen not to be offered the job, however, it's easy to say how thrilled you'd be to come back as an extra player.)

There are a few clever ways in which you can manoeuvre. A confidential disclosure to the principal that a higher-ranking job might attract you, and you could find that back-desk job transformed into one farther up the section. (After all, they haven't had time yet to figure out that you don't fit in any better than the other members they've already picked.) A confidential d. to the principal that you'd agree to take the job if only you hadn't got to sit next to X, who last tried to play well back in the 1970s but who still earns three times your annual declaration, might cause him to alter the section order out of sympathy (assuming he agrees about X, whom he's probably been trying to unload for decades). There are related excuses for not accepting a job, including a child (make sure you have one) who can't leave her present school even in order for you to move to the job of your dreams. But there is also the data you should have gathered during the period — which can be extensive — of your trial. There is no point in telling Alf Garnett's younger brother that your voluntary work on behalf of Sri Lankan asylum seekers would prevent your moving to Glasgow, even if this is true. (Orchestras really do seem to cover all types, believe me.)

There is yet another option: if selected, you can take the job. 'There's old George set up for life,' your friends will say enviously, and your enemies, particularly those who are also viola-players, will be pleasanter to you than they have been in ages. The extras will flatter you, and you will cement a few friendships among your fellow players. But after a few years a dreadful ennui will set in, a miasma of dull grey sessions in unwindowed rooms, of concert after concert, of the same set of faces growing older and paler even as you look at them. You will buy a house with a mortgage larger than you can afford, your marriage will atrophy and your children hardly see you. You will grow to loathe your oboe or your violin with a hatred in inverse relation to how many times you can bear to pick it up without mention of a buy-out fee. You will reject offers to play chamber music with friends, and wonder what all that effort was good for in the end. And you will still earn less and work harder than your neighbour in accountancy and your brother in a solicitor's office. You're now a real musician, one of the most successful in the country. Congratulations, people will tell you. You made it.

RULE 25: Rules for principals. So you get to be a principal. Would you mind not leaping about with joy—or not in public, anyway. You'd be surprised how few principals are genuinely popular and/or respected, even (or perhaps especially) within their own sections. There are a few simple tricks, however, which should preclude outright mutiny in yours, whether you're king-for-a-day-on-a-choral-society-date or the genuine article.

The first of these is: if in doubt, don't. Don't attempt to control your number four's habit of a lifetime, whether this is coming in a fraction early or hanging on a fraction late. You're probably dead right, but a public correction is unforgiveable.

Don't alter a bowing unless you must, especially on those one-rehearsal, chicken-tikka-masala, bash-through-the-concert, and hit-the-M1-running affairs. If you do, imagining it being transmitted respectfully down the section, allow me to enlighten you as to what actually happens.

Second desk will mark it in correctly, and third desk incorrectly, which is partly the fault of second desk's not making it clear. Fourth desk will manage to spot third desk's error; and will helpfully tell them, which will irritate third desk no end. Fourth desk will have been far too busy correcting third desk to inform fifth desk, who are anyway chatting with the basses; and by then the conductor is glaring at the entire section, sheep and goats alike, for wasting time. (Fifth desk will never get the bowing in, but, as this is traditional, there is nothing that can be done about it.)

Don't waste the orchestra's time by waffling on to fellow principals about phrasing or inter-pretation. It almost always looks pretentious anyway. The exception to this rule is if yours is a period-instrument orchestra, where such time-wasting is expected and even encouraged. There is always an unofficial pecking order in authentic orchestras (depending upon the raw level of authenticity, sometimes known as the vegan index) and you must unquestionably defer to those ranked higher than you on this scale, wherever they are sitting, in or out of your particular section. In other words, unless you are quite intolerably meat-eschewing, you will always be required to give way to somebody more anally retentive than yourself. This is the essence of period-instrument democracy, herbal remedies and organic wheatgerm.

But back to the issue at hand. Should your section—Heaven forfend—rush or drag or otherwise misbehave, do not automatically tear strips off its tail-end. Chances are it was someone else's fault altogether, and the blameless few will never forgive you. If you, on the other hand, mistakenly lead your section down the garden path, confess your sin immediately and publicly. Do not say that the sun was in your eyes, or that, had the violas been more together, it would not have happened. Just apologise, and concentrate harder next time.

Do not attempt to teach members of your section how to play. Some of them may well have been working longer than you have been alive. Simply point out, for example, that it 'seemed' to go 'a bit quicker than marked' at letter B, and leave it at that. Turning around with such a light observation more than once an hour is not to be recommended, however anxious you are to share your scintillating expertise or to impress the orchestra leader. The best principals lead simply by the nature of their leading. If your section members happen to be yearning for a refresher violin lesson (unlikely but conceivable) then there are times and places and teachers of their own choosing, not those imposed upon them. You can be sure that, docile as they may seem, your section will be judging you just as narrowly as you are perceived to be judging them. Morale is best ensured by the fostering of a team spirit, not the encouraging of a 'them and us' mentality. It is also worth remembering the possibility that, one year or other, someone you used to lead might wind up leading *you*.

*Your brief as principal does
not extend to other people's sections.*

Tragic as it may seem, your brief as principal does not extend to other people's sections (with the exception of period-instrument ensembles). If, as principal second, you perceive a rushing in the violas, the correct move is to share a quiet coffee with the viola principal in the break. There is a widespread belief, and one fiercely resented by the double bass fraternity, that they are serfs of the cello section. The principal bass is still the principal bass, and would thank you to remember it. (This is particularly true if, as is likely, he is bigger than you are.) The only person allowed to throw his weight around every section is the orchestra leader, and even the leader can be resented if he or she throws it too often.

Try to treat each member of your section equally. Be as courteous to the grizzled old veteran as to the comely young thing. Try not to pass audible judgements on their relative worth, and do not attempt to alter their seating, unless you are being irresistibly bribed to do so. You may — if you must — alter the existing extra list, but at least attempt to do it subtly, easing people out or in, rather than simply dumping them. Wherever possible, blame Higher Powers. Cultivate an air of regretful sympathy, and let your fixer or conductor take the stick for the order in which your section is booked and seated.

If you can do all this, play wonderful solos and keep a solid grip on your sanity, you're a better man than I am, Gunga Din.

RULE 26: So, you agree to become an orchestral contractor or fixer. Good luck to you. You have landed a job which combines seeming popularity with genuine detestation, real power with rotten remuneration, and a lot of hard work with the exercise of the smallest conceivable amount of creative judgement. Why these jobs remain sought-after is a mystery, but they tend to attract bright young things who imagine it glamorous to work in the arts and clever clogs who perceive it as a crafty way out of playing for a living.

Which of course it is, up to a point, hence the resentment of the playing masses (more or less neatly disguised as charming friendliness). It's hard not to feel bemused at being hired or fired by someone who might (or jolly well might not) have achieved Grade 7 on the recorder; it's irritating enough worrying about being approved by anyone at all. Fixers should (by law, really) be extrovert, kindly souls with an agreeable word for everybody, just in order to set people's minds at rest — and, of course, some of them are, including, by strange coincidence, every single fixer known to me personally.

However, and despite this fact, I have heard of numerous incidents involving fixers: fixers who arbitrarily ditch players for rejecting their sexual advances, fixers who oblige their friends at the expense of long-term players' livelihoods, fixers who manipulate principals for their own ends, or who otherwise behave in a manner displeasing to interested parties. Fellow freelance players seem to spend half their lives moaning about fixers.

Personally, I find such complaints extraordinary. If the rules for fixing were better understood, then no one would find anything to wonder at. For those considering a career in fixing, those still at music college or those disadvantaged by ignorance, I submit them here.

As a fixer you must start by booking the people, in order specified, whom you are obliged to book by the principal concerned. Progress, after that, to (a) people, not excluding your recognised partner, with whom you are presently sharing a bed, (b) people with whom you wish you were, however briefly, sharing a bed, (c) people you are particularly friendly with whose playing will not disgrace you, (d) people you are p.f.w. whose playing might disgrace you, (e) people you may not know or like who are outstanding players, (f) people you may not know or like who are good players, and finally (g) the dregs of the earth.

As I have reason to believe that these particular rules will be rigorously attended to, you had better memorise them, whether or not you ever intend to fix. They will enable you to understand the behaviour, however seemingly eccentric, of this amiable profession, and prevent you from becoming, however briefly, a 'fixer-bore', or one who blames everything, up to and including the destruction of the Amazonian rainforest, upon the fixer. Remember, these gallant men and women, representing all that is best and brightest in British cultural life, project in their unshakeable ideals all that brought us into the profession in the first place, all that is best summed up by the poet Burns when he wrote...

(*That's enough fixer-oiling. Ed.*)

RULE 27: Rules for conductors. Whole books have been written about how to conduct, which are to a book completely useless, as they address issues of technique or even (God help us) musicianship. The rules of conducting — the real rules, the ones that produce good morale and better results — can be elucidated not by conductors, whether great or otherwise, but by foot-soldiers like myself, the cogs in the machine. So put your stick down and shut up, for a moment, while the last bloody cellist explains in words of one syllable

Conductors – it helps to be of East European ancestry.

why your orchestras hate you, and what you can do about it.

In the first place, conductors are loathed because they earn too much. A typically eminent conductor earns, per concert, about a quarter as much as the typical full-time player earns all year. For some reason I cannot attempt to explain this is perceived as subtly unfair by the players concerned. There is no shortage of wailing and gnashing of teeth even when the conductor is a genius, but as there are only about three conducting geniuses alive at any one time (this is another little-known rule), the irritation of said players can be extreme.

Then we come to the rather more numerous ranks of non-geniuses. The average concert-goer has no conception of how many conducting performances are salvaged by the orchestra, simply in order to preserve the players' jobs or the group's reputation. Some of the biggest conducting names — often, but not exclusively, those who 'made it' as soloists rather than conductors in the first place — are lethal weapons when let loose on a symphony orchestra. Fortunately, established orchestras can play standard repertoire by rote, and have a character to preserve. Otherwise there would be blood on the stage.

But to return to the conductor. Bad enough, then, to be squirming underneath the musical heel of someone earning many times your fee, but when the performance is a success in spite of him (it's almost never a 'her') mutiny can set in. Be aware, as a conductor, that you live on borrowed time—and borrowed goodwill. Without wheedling or toadying to the orchestra (they will despise you still more) you must get them on your side. Like a fixer, you will receive artificial expressions of support enough; the trick is to translate these into the genuine article.

If you are hard-working and competent, this is not so impossible. If you can learn your scores, use your rehearsal time efficiently, keep a clear beat, and give adequate and unfussy cues, there is hope. If you can manage a touch of black humour, you may even find it possible to nurture the falsehood that 'we're all in this together'. And if you can actually find a morsel of genuine musical inspiration, then (regardless of how badly you mess up all the other rules) good players will still fight to play under you. But never forget that you are earning a fortune, massaging your ego and supporting all four of your previous wives on the backs of the harder-worked, unrewarded and poorly remunerated people in front of you. Any suggestion of arrogance will turn them against you forever, and may conceivably lose you work, because even the passionate support of record companies can be counterbalanced by the determination of an entire self-governing orchestra to be shot of you.

Many of the preceding rules ought also to apply to you. Like a good principal, you should let your actions do the talking, resisting the impulse to natter on about interpretation, even when the press is present. Like a good leader, you shouldn't always appear to be targeting the rear of a section when giving your criticisms (or the front when doling out bouquets). Like a savvy extra, you should take note of some players' little hobbies and foibles, thus effortlessly achieving a reputation for good temper and good fellowship. You should stand your round, even if it means forking out for an entire orchestra at the end of a tour. (They will never forget it. Never.)

You should appear to respect a principal player's musical opinions even if you secretly despise them. Try to make a point of occasionally soliciting (and even taking) advice from a principal; you've no idea what gratification this produces. Don't neglect the cultivation of those members who, through sheer force of personality or position on the players' board, are more powerful than their position in the orchestra might suggest. Never forget to thank an orchestra for a good performance. Never forget to thank an orchestra for *any* performance. Be generous with private words of support to your principals, especially those under particular pressure for any reason. Go for substance over style; orchestras have an inbuilt distaste for meaningless, crowd-pleasing posturing. Neither a cringer nor a bullier be, unless you want to be either ridiculed or regarded with secret hatred. Don't lose your temper, except perhaps with the organisers of a tour who have failed to treat your players with due consideration. (This last is highly effective.) Never withdraw from a concert with a minor orchestra in order to deputise with a more famous one. Never abuse one orchestra to another (the first orchestra will inevitably hear about it). If you are obliged to fire an established player — and, in the long run, the evidence suggests it's probably not worth it— make sure you garner near-unanimous support in advance. And don't have favourites.

This last is, naturally enough, impossible. We all have favourites. But conductors should keep their private feelings to themselves. There are few quicker routes to oblivion than always preferring to talk, gossip or simply hang around with only a handful of your players, whether sex comes into it or not. The distrust, disapproval and resentment of the rest will never compensate for any momentary support or satisfaction your favoured few will give you.

The problems conductors have with orchestras are almost all traceable to one of the following causes: over-familiarity with player or players, loss of control with a player or players, power struggles with management, or arrogant behaviour that erodes an orchestra's natural respect.

But don't be too cast down. Surprisingly few problems are caused by the conductor's being an unmusical, boring bastard with a rotten stick technique, largely because most players have given up expecting anything much better. There may be hope for your career yet, particularly if (a) you are already a world-famous soloist, (b) you have been born into an eminent musical family (regardless of ability), (c) you are a handsome manipulator of image-makers and recording company executives, or (d) you are of East European ancestry. It doesn't exactly hurt to be good, but being good is no guarantee that you'll get anywhere. Which is one of life's universal truths, come to think of it, and not a Rule at all.

RULE 28: Those who can teach; those who can avoid teaching, do. In practice — pay attention at the back, for God's sake: this means *you* — almost everyone teaches, from the mighty soloist to the full-time peripatetic. Everybody especially teaches who at any point maintains, with elevated nose, that they certainly don't intend to *teach*, I mean, *honestly* — and that they personally were Born to Perform. So there's no point hoping that you'll be such a stunning player that you won't have time to run masterclasses at the Guildhall twice a year. Minor soloists earn a substantial proportion of their income from teaching, as do some major soloists. And all soloists make up point zero zero one percent of working musicians anyway.

So, there is no escape. You are going to teach. The world needs classical musicians like a hole in the ozone layer, but teachers will always be required. The tragic truth is that, while little Sophie's parents would never consider attending an orchestral concert themselves, they tend to discover it necessary for Sophie's middle-class credentials that she sweat blood over the flute or the piano. All of which corresponds interestingly to the situation in Regency times of young ladies being obliged to learn the harp or pianoforte in order to attach future husbands and to emphasise the gentility of their breeding, only to quit playing as soon as decently possible after marriage. (The main difference today is that the young people generally quit a long sight before marriage, or as soon as decently possible after leaving the parental nest.) Now the jolly side of this is that the gifted orchestral flautist needn't starve while awaiting his big break. His main danger is of being brought up on manslaughter charges after

the tenth parent of the day marvels aloud that he isn't already adorning the Philharmonia wind section.

And here one must pause to pay tribute to those legions of musicians who battle daily with the menaces the rest of us face only a few hours a week: the 'real' teachers, the (mainly) teachers, and those front-line troops, the peripatetics. Here in Britain there are thousands upon thousands of these brave souls, some of them well-stricken in years, others barely out of music college, striving manfully and womanfully to bring breath control, bow technique or pedal power to the masses. Their wan complexions and trembling fingers tell the tale: of David who dared and Petunia who failed, and of Petunia's Mum, who tore strips off Petunia's teacher even though she Had Been Warned. In the opinion of many (though very possibly not Petunia's Mum) these are classical music's unsung heroes. As I write, they are at this very moment in dingy uncarpeted holes up and down the land adjusting Emily's bow arm for the forty-fifth time, or saying, with a patience that would make angels weep: 'I'm sorry, Charles, but if your mother won't buy you another set of reeds, I won't be able to teach you bassoon anymore.'

There but for the Grace of God go all of us; and the way things are going, there go most of us anyway.

But what does teaching mean in practice? (Using the term loosely, because between homework, brother Joey tripping over the viola, a mysterious ailment acquired while tree-climbing and a really striking lack of interest, most pupils don't practise anyway.) It means patience, nerve, determination, imagination, understanding and concentration. Going one-on-one with young instrumentalists is among the most exhausting jobs there is, even with a talented student, and it is desperately ill-rewarded in terms of pay, security and status. All teachers are somewhat exploited, but instrumental music teachers are at the bottom of the heap, right down there with fellow sufferers in art, drama and physical education. You will feel as lonely as a soloist, as overdrawn as a chamber-music player, and as musically drained as a full-time orchestra member. You will be required to give energy and enthusiasm until it feels like blood. No soloistic cosseting will be awarded you, and no chamber-music kudos. You will miss out on the fellow feeling that exists between orchestra members; and it is likely that not even the student you are teaching will care. Why on earth does anybody do it?

Because there is an occasional moment that makes it worth it, and I'm not just talking about such rare instances as when a teacher friend of mine talked a boarding school student out of suicide. There are less significant but still genuine sources of gratification in teaching. Not only the solid satisfaction of steering a student from beginner into a youth orchestra, but the real pleasure, which the one-to-one system permits, of watching people grow personally as well as musically. The feeling when you open your front door (expecting the meter-reader) to find that they've come back from university to see you, not having so much as dusted off their instrument all year, but still wanting to meet their former teacher again. The knowledge that you've meant something in their lives, even influenced them, one way or another. Whenever they see an orchestra, they will think of you: audiences are crammed with other people's ex-students. And, who knows?, they may be standing at the kitchen sink, decades from now, and find a snatch of music drifting through their heads. You will be as present to them then as if you were immortal. You may even have enriched their lives with some kind of love of music — of even more than music. As Gerald White Johnson wrote: 'A man who has tried to play Mozart and failed, through that vain effort comes into position better to understand the man who tried to paint the Sistine Madonna, and did.'

There are also worse things in life than teaching, which is just as well. Got that, you at the back? Pass it on, then, to future generations, pass it on.

Rules for teaching

If a pupil really longs to learn a specific piece, then let him have a go, however out of reach it might seem. He'll discover soon enough that your doubts were justified; and he also might learn something from it (such as that his teacher, though past it, can still sometimes be right). He might even astonish you by playing it: pupils only really work at something they're genuinely interested in — sex, for instance. And we all know that some pieces take a lifetime to learn anyway.

If a pupil doesn't want to do exams, don't oblige him to. The exam system has some good points, and many less good points: pupils should be allowed, and in some cases encouraged, to opt out. As for the over-ambitious pupil (or, more likely, parent), as long as the risk of failure is made clear, he should be entitled to try his strength: it's an odd exam that he'll take nothing away from, even if he fails it. It's crucial too to stress that even what students perceive to be the dizzy heights of Grade 8 means comparatively little in the grand scheme of things. (I was demonstrating some years ago to a youngster who commented, 'You must have got Grade 8!' 'No,' was my possibly unique response, as one who grew up in America, 'I didn't even get Grade 1.') What Grade 8 really means is that you're not a beginner anymore.

Attempt to adapt your lesson plan to the pupil's state of mind. You know yourself how useless it is to try to feel creative when you're low or exhausted; this is the time to plough through studies or adjust technique. Always try to find something to praise: if the child's intonation and bow-arm are corrected unremittingly for an hour, she can't be blamed for deciding she's rubbish and might as well chuck the whole thing. If a generally conscientious pupil hasn't practised, spend the lesson playing duos or working on sight-reading. The carrot and the stick need to be very delicately balanced. Some players — adults as well as children — require constant encouragement; and a lesson consisting mainly of criticisms is enough to discourage anybody.

Try not to spend half the lesson grabbing the kid's clarinet. Jolly as it is that you can play all the

Grade 7 pieces perfectly, it is, after all, only to be expected, and there is a limit to the amount that can be taught by demonstration. Coming physically to grips with the instrument the child is playing is mainly useful if you suspect it (rather than her) of some inbuilt deficiency. Control your urge to hog the lesson yourself, however drastically short of practice you may be.

Foster a notion of partnership. One famous and virtuosic teacher I studied with used to exclaim when I said I needed a lesson, 'So do I!' No serious musician ever stops learning; and we're all in the same boat, which, incidentally, is sinking.

Stage fright is the great imponderable of teaching. It produces the Little Jerk who Hardly Deserved a Pass but Pulled Off a Distinction on the Day, as well as the desperately hard-working and able creature who falls apart and fails to do herself justice. Exams are inherently unfair. It may help little Jessie to hear about the weird and wonderful marks that you have experienced or heard of, or it may not. Certainly you might suggest to pupils that (a) you personally have confidence in their abilities, whether you do or not, (b) exams are most importantly learning experiences, and (c) you are personally proud of what they've accomplished, whether the system nourishes their little psyches or not. Beyond this, and short of lacing their apple juice with beta-blockers, there's not a lot you can do.

Exams are vastly overrated by children, whose best friend seems inevitably to have already achieved Grade 8 distinction on flute. If a student is traumatised, the safest course is to withdraw him from the firing line. Some orchestras or summer courses don't require exams; and quite often life (especially for kids) contains enough in-built competition without seeking out still more. Exams are most useful for lazy and unimaginative players who require a 'reason' to practise and for parents short of material to brag about at Blackheath dinner parties. The best rule for parents, pupils and teachers alike is not to take them very seriously.

RULE 29: Rules for foreign tours. The safest rule for foreign tours is not to tour, but as with so many rules, it will always be broken. Your friends will suggest you have your head examined if you reject touring, the pressures of work being what they are. And if you are in a full-time London symphony orchestra, ballet orchestra or opera orchestra, a certain proportion of your life will be composed of touring anyway.

They vary frantically of course, from the once-before-bust Italian jaunt (for which you never get quite completely paid) to the glossily sponsored London orchestra extravaganza, which is still a lot less glamorous than it sounds. The truth about even the best orchestra tours is that you see more of identikit hotels and airports than local sights and culture, but what did you expect, you're not being paid to have a good time, are you?

Well, you are a bit, to be honest. Even the two-day trip to Boulogne feels different from the Royal Festival Hall, and despite endless coach journeys, long queues, rushed meals and 5 a.m. alarm calls it is still more amusing to tour than not to tour (unless again you're in a really major orchestra, which gets too much of all good things). You are almost bound to see something interesting, even if it's only the conductor getting off with the second flute. And you will inevitably get to know an orchestra better on tour than working — even over a period of years — at its home base.

Which is not to say that orchestra members behave normally on tours. The only people whose behaviour is not affected by touring are those chess-playing, rose-breeding throwbacks to a gentler age sometimes known as 'pond life'. These are usually has-beens in the strings, older members, long-suffering and good-natured, accountants or historians manqué. They nap upon arrival and flee to their bedrooms straight after a concert. They sometimes play deplorably, and in some cases always did, competition not having been especially fierce in the 1960s; but, as few people can ever hear them, it doesn't greatly matter.

The rest of the orchestra, however, does behave differently on tour. Freed from the shackles of arguing with their spouses, avoiding their teenagers and not being able to park around London, some seize the opportunity to increase their acquaintance among the bartending community, enhancing their ongoing research project into local beers and conceiving the night ill-spent if sleeping features in more than two hours of it. These are the toughies, with lower strings, brass and percussion predominating. On tour they resemble boys — boys let out of school early and determined to make the most of it.

Others — mainly women, for some reason — are indefatigable tourists. These worthies scarcely let their feet touch land before they advance, phrase-books at the ready, keen to imbibe whatever cultural enrichment is on offer, even if the total amount of free time before rehearsal is scarcely enough to enable lesser mortals to grab a meal. They are sometimes ridiculed by the rest of the orchestra, who are secretly overawed by such

*Main touring interests are food,
drinking and sex.*

an excess of zeal and breeding. But the truth is that, for the majority, the main touring interests are food, drinking and sex, in that order.

The food is imperative. Beware, conductors, the ill-fed band: Christians had a matier relationship with the Coliseum lions than you will have with a hungry orchestra. Properly fed and watered, and accorded reasonable accommodation, an orchestra is tolerant and tolerable on a tour. Let the system even slightly break down, however, and the growling begins, as from the very centre of the earth (generally the double basses). For many in the orchestra, the entertainment stops at the food. To them, the browsing and (moderate) sluicing *are* the tour.

Most of the rest, notably the toughies, stop at the drink. This is less because of disinclination for sex than because, by the time they've been ejected from the bar, the spirit may be willing, but the flesh is as putty. It's also probably true that in mainly masculine bands the odds against success ensure that the more certain consolation of alcohol prevails. Touring is one of the principal causes of alcoholism in orchestras — the loneliness, the purposeless hanging about and the lack of outside interests being the culprits.

Finally you get those who behave differently on

tours mainly or exclusively due to interest in sex. I am not referring here to those established couples — whether in wedlock, out of wedlock, or in wedlock to other people entirely — that exist in every orchestra, but to those individuals whose main leisure activity seems to be coercing or persuading other people (not excluding conductors, management or soloists) to go to bed with them. At ordinary times a tiny proportion of any orchestra, this group on tour can vary from 10% to 33.3333333% of a touring party, depending on length of tour and amount of free time available. It is what I call the Munich syndrome, partly because it has a satisfyingly scientific ring, and partly because of an experience I once had in Munich.

I was on a hit-and-run orchestral tour which involved a free afternoon and, the following day, a free evening. I spent the free afternoon blamelessly with a male acquaintance, exploring galleries and choosing inexpensive presents for nephews and nieces. When he avoided me the next day, I inquired what was wrong. With evident embarrassment my friend said that we had been 'observed together shopping' the previous day and that he was too worried in case his wife heard to continue to be friendly to me. (I may add that we are both known to be happily married: such is the gossip quotient added on a tour.)

The next evening I happened to have dinner in our hotel with another intelligent fellow, to whom I related the tale. Agreeing that ''twas strange, 'twas passing strange, 'twas pitiful, 'twas wondrous pitiful', he proceeded, with neither prior warning nor recommended flirtation time, to endeavour to pick me up. My day was complete when a brass player to whom I had never been introduced — and who was in no condition to complete an introduction anyway — came knocking on my door at 3 a.m. desiring comfort and consolation and a few things besides. (When I discovered the next day that some six or seven other women players had also been approached in the middle of the night, I couldn't decide if that made it worse or better.)

What the Munich syndrome tells us is this: that people will believe any gossip circulating on a tour, and that they are often right to do so. The mildest-seeming soul can be turned by the touring experience into a raving Casanova; and you can trust almost nobody to tell the truth. To top it off, rows and misunderstandings also reach heights undreamt of in the calmer climes of London. The slightest incident — a disagreement about bowings, a rumour about what the principal oboe said about the principal horn — can assume mammoth significance on a tour, especially at mid-point, the psychological low of the trip. Then the whole world seems to recede except for the handful of paranoid schizophrenics you are tied to, and every day seems to last a lifetime.

Which is all immensely interesting of course, but also very wearing. I recommend the following sub-rules for tours:

Get away from it all. Don't be afraid to be thought dull or anti-social. Spend an afternoon exploring on your own, or even just reading in your hotel room. This will increase your sense of perspective almost as much as phoning home, and is very much cheaper.

Be sociable, but don't overdo it. If you're found at the bar as it closes at 2 a.m., your colleagues can hardly be blamed for imagining that you're asking for it, especially in their probable condition. Don't be the first to leave the orchestra party, but don't be the last either.

Make a real effort not to become a signed-up member of one of the many cliques. You stand a better chance of general popularity (and a better chance of avoiding getting over-involved with any one person) if you spread yourself around more thinly. A baroque violinist I know used to make a serious effort to eat one meal with every member of the tour, which is a worthier ambition than some I could mention, though seriously impractical with a full symphony orchestra.

Discover or develop some non-musical interest, whether it be water-colours, local cheeses, gothic cathedrals or European motorway networks. These kinds of outlets can be sanity-savers.

Don't have an affair with the conductor, however dashing, lonely or generally misunderstood he might be. The odds against his actually abandoning wife and children for you have been calculated by our experts at 999:1, and every other outcome is traditionally at your eventual expense. The same advice goes for the fixer. Cases where players have come unstuck in this fashion are both too numerous and libellous to be rehearsed here. If you insist on having an affair on tour, at least try to choose someone of your own orchestral status, so that the upshot is less likely to be detrimental to you.

It may be tempting, particularly if your principal is excessively talented or possesses a foreign accent, to confirm your position as favoured extra or member of his section by giving in. The result is nearly always catastrophic. The only sensible excuse for permitting a principal to seduce you is in order to gain a full-time position, and, even then, only if you're pretty confident you want that particular job for life, because absolutely everyone will know. They may even 'know' if nothing ever actually happened, orchestral gossip being what it is, but hey, whoever said that life was fair?

RULE 30: Rules for recordings. These vary from the film session — which is about the only really well-paid work orchestral players get — to the live concert for Radio 3 where the additional fee would be hard put to stretch to more than a couple of rounds in the pub. There is nothing very instructive to be said about them, although there is a good deal to be said *for* them, especially for light music sessions, notwithstanding clicky headphones and oceans of semibreves.

Some players become very nervy about live broadcasts, though just about anything can happen during these; and no one seems to get too fussed. Perfecting a CD, however, especially under tight time restrictions, can be a truly terrifying experience—especially in a chamber-sized group, where there can be absolutely no doubt about who hit his bow against the stand during the first and probably only take that satisfied the piano soloist. Standards are so exacting for CDs that the tiniest extraneous sound will upset the producer. (I was once embarrassed by interference being tracked down to my silver earrings.) Financial considerations mean that swathes of music have to be got in the can on a tight schedule, and conductors and even normally equable record producers get seriously ratty as the sand slips through the hourglass and the polish still isn't there. The tight politeness of their exchanges ('Great, terrific, *almost* there, but can the oboe's D go up at all and the basses not drag bar four, and there's still that rather rancid F# in the firsts —') gives way to more pungent language ('It sounds like a pile of shit'), which is why a secret telephone line from producer to conductor is frankly such a good idea.

All too rarely, dummy sessions for TV or film come along for the ardent freelance. Everything to do with film is wearyingly time-consuming for people used to attacking the 'Eroica' on two rehearsals: they can't seem to shoot a beetle on a ledge without endless technical consultations, not to mention debates about the motivation of the beetle — but it's certainly different. And it can be quite a liberating experience to saw away at your fiddle or squawk through your reed without caring a hang about the output, as they're getting the LSO to over-dub anyway. The pay is good, and the whole business will impress your relatives and friends out of all proportion to its interest. And if and when you finally manage to spot yourself on screen you'll be amazed at how short the scene you were put through actually lasts.

Being invited to play for TV or film.

In the 80s, my then diary service was instructed to fix an entire orchestra for *Electric Dreams*, the first, and, so far as I am aware, only representative of that genre in which a computer falls in love with a cellist (don't ask). At any rate, at one point our actress/cellist heroine, for reasons which still remain obscure, squeezes into a lift with her priceless instrument, which is clothed in the feeblest of canvas cases, whereupon I personally can be heard intoning my immortal line, 'Somebody's been skipping their Jane Fonda exercise classes!' (No, I didn't get any extra money for my line, and no, I don't know why I got picked, either.) The lead actress having carefully positioned the cello where maximum impact can be assured, the next sound one hears is that of crushed cheapo Romanian cello in the lift door, followed by a deathless silence, as our heroine moves slowly out of the lift, clutching her ex-cello, as if rendered unnaturally dumb with sorrow.

They shot that idiotic scene about six times, or until there were rumblings of outrage when we learned that these were real cellos being massacred. They then declared an end to the slaughter, and to my footnote in film history.

Happy days!

RULE 31: Rules for background music. The emphasis here is entirely on presentation. While you can get by looking unkempt or dowdy in an orchestra, manner and appearance is all in this field of work, which is why mediocre groups consisting entirely of lovely young girls get so much of it. Men's clothes must be irreproachable, and women must either look positively divine singly or find matching outfits if more than one female is involved. Basically, and however offensive you may find the concept, you are there to be looked at. This is only partly because, once the do gets going, even the most dedicated guest will be hard put to hear you. What you are selling here is image. The corporation (mother of the bride, owner of the stately home) is subliminally saying, 'See how cultured we are.' This image is not best promoted, however stunning your oboe's timbre, in unironed shirts or Oxfam dresses, with your music slopped all over the floor.

Rules for background gigs

Be sensitive. Not only to fluctuations in the number of guests — don't ghetto-blast a handful of courting couples — but also to fluctuations in mood. Once people start letting their hair down, Mozart is out and jazz is in. And once the bread rolls start flying, as they did at one corporate dinner I was playing for, you are all entitled to ankle off for the better preservation of your instruments.

Be aware of the nuances contained in your choices. 'Yesterday' or 'Smoke gets in your eyes (when you fall in love)' are not reckoned ideal for weddings, while a wealthy Jewish host is likely to be underwhelmed by 'If I was a rich man' from *Fiddler*. 'Cabaret' goes down badly with Germans, for some reason, and 'When I'm 64' is not brill for charity do's at old folks' homes.

Be tactful. More inane remarks are addressed to background musicians than to any other single group. Everyone will want to know if you're playing a Strad, how you get the cello under your chin, whether you have the theme from *The X-Files* (you don't), what you do for a living, how long you have played together (this inevitably when your usual leader is down with cholera and your cellist off on his only film session of the year, and it's in fact your debut with this personnel, so lie through your teeth), and whether they might have a go at your instrument (run). Being charming is actually part of the job here, so that the mother of the bride will get compliments not only on your performance but on your agree-ableness. Keep smiling, while reminding yourself simultaneously of your overdraft and of the cheque that is even now in the post.

Don't drink to excess or allow anyone else in your group to do so. It is cringingly embarrassing to be obliged to bring *Czardas* to a premature end due to your leader's falling over his fingerboard. Granted, free Pimms or good wine can be tough to resist, but such a proceeding will neither endear you to your host, nor imbue your technique with the sparkle you fondly imagine. This is one time when it pays to be a cheap date.

RULE 32: Playing in shows. This used to be regarded as something people did when orchestra work was slow, but that was before orchestras started looking such a bad long-term bet themselves. Positions in shows are now highly sought-after, despite the fact that it's a repetitive job playing what is usually less than deathless music. Most of the regulars seem to have a real love-hate relationship with their show: they live in fear and trembling lest it be taken off, but will do almost anything in order to avoid playing in it. (They also have a love-hate relationship with West End musicals generally. The one they happen to play in is invariably tuneful, moving, and a real breath of fresh air. Everyone else's is just another hack effort cluttering up a characterful theatre that used to do proper plays.)

When their show does come off, these players invariably mooch about muttering darkly about bankruptcy but somehow always manage to land another one, usually through the people they employed as extras while their previous show was on, so no surprises there.

There is something, however, in the atmosphere of an orchestra pit, whether theatre or ballet etc. that I should perhaps mention. Orchestral politics, neurotic as they are at the best of times, seem to be particularly vicious in these places. Like otherwise civilised rats deprived of light, regular pit players can exhibit bizarre behaviour patterns. A friend of mine from our days at the same music college who plays on Broadway gives an illustration of my point. The usual extras being unavailable, she was asked to lead a show for a couple of days. The musical director, impressed, asked her for a third show as leader. It was on this occasion that a strange incident occurred. During her most exposed violin solo, the foot of the player behind her inexplicably, accidentally, tragically slipped, shoving my friend's chair some inches forward and completely disrupting her solo. The m.d. got the message and my friend was not asked again.

This is an illustration of another little-known rule: Try not to play too well. (Or: Beware of rats in pits.)

*Baroque orchestras –
marry money.*

RULE 33: Rules for baroque orchestras. And here I must spring to the defence of these worthy souls, so often derided as wincingly precious, technically underwhelming and obsessively concerned with the examination of their musicological navels. For a start, those who complain are often jealous of the reviews the 'cobweb brigade' get, plus the extra (danger) money they receive. (In the past they were also jealous of the baroque groups' recording contracts, but since most of the decent early repertoire has now been recorded, those days of milk and honey have pretty much died a death.)

Secondly, you too might find your normally sunny character a trifle warped if you had to deal with such recalcitrant objects as a baroque oboe or a natural horn. Gut strings alone are notably character-building, as they go out of tune at the flicker of a temperature or humidity change. Indeed the whole of the period experience is further evidence, if such were needed, that we are not put on earth in order to enjoy ourselves. No, we are born to struggle and endure, and in some cases (the early cor anglais springs nimbly to mind) we are born quite frankly to struggle.

Thirdly, it is such a small world that the average modern-instrument player can have no notion of how tediously incestuous it can be. It is possible for the BBC Symphony to be pretty clueless about what the Covent Garden band is up to; but in the stone-age scene, the same players (especially those especially gifted, or especially gifted at convincing fixers that they are especially gifted) pop up everywhere. And these orchestras can be so tiny — mere chamber groups sometimes — that it is a credit to the natural ingenuity of human nature that they can contain so many varieties of sheer, unadulterated bitchiness.

Some people in the profession have been known to suggest that this is a function of having so many more women than men in the ancient brigade, but I maintain that there is something about massed ranks of either women *or* men that is rancid, orchestrally speaking. The ideal would probably be a balance, as there is in the rest of life, but then, even attempting balance can be unfair, especially as — for whatever reason — women do seem to particularly excel at early music. A fixer once apologised for not having asked me on a baroque tour because 'We've got to have a few straight men!' Now for an orgy I could have followed her line of thinking — been with her, absolutely — but for four days in Italy?

The special rules for baroque orchestras are as follows:

It is always a good idea to show up with the correct period equipment, but don't expect everyone else to. The starrier the player the less period his equipment will be, is the rule of thumb, but you're just starting out, so at least try to get it right.

It is an excellent idea to study with really good period players. This often acts as an informal audition, and can advance you in your career. (Didn't work for me, though. My teacher died.) You can also learn a good deal by going to concerts of the very best baroque groups and checking out how many violinists are cheating with shoulder-rests (ditto cellists with spikes). There are various courses which specialise in these techniques, mainly run by well-established players, and there are some crucial books to imbibe, some actually written in the stone age (Leopold Mozart) as well as more recent (Judy Tarling) written for the benefit of people who really love the music.

And the music, of course, is wonderful. It almost makes up for all the rest just to play Bach, Mozart or Beethoven in period style. It's true that only a handful of people can make period instruments sound tolerable on their own (the correct timbre being that of a proper instrument with a raging head-cold), but, put together in an orchestra, and with the fleetness, spirit and phrasing suited to early music, it can sound marvellous and feel terrific.

One last rule for baroque (or indeed any) orchestras: Marry money. For a start, all those instruments can really add up, and you'll probably need an extra room in which to store them. Also, and follow me closely here, at some point or other you will want a mortgage. That garret that currently seems so divine in South Kensington you will someday outgrow. And mortgage lenders as a race seem to have a perverse preference that at least one mortgagee can count on an income worth multiplying.

Indeed, this seems such an obvious rule that it amazes me to observe how rarely it is actually followed. So many musicians marry fellow musicians, careless of the fact that they'll hardly ever see each other (or see far too much of each other if in the same orchestra), that they'll always have two insecure incomes instead of only one, that evening childcare will be even more hellish than it is for non-musos, and that (far from having someone who 'understands what makes you tick') you'll have some other orchestra's politics and hassles to worry about, as well as your own. No, no. What I advise is that you trot down to Harrods pronto and pick yourself up a nice sheik, or sheikess, and forget how wonderfully your adored plays Chopin on the piano/Mahler on the horn/Brahms on the violin. Some day you'll thank me for it.

RULE 34: Rules for amateur orchestras. There are little nuggets of amateur excellence all over the country, and the attitude of people who are entirely playing for love can be immensely refreshing. These are the rehearsals where second violinists come with scores under their arms, where third trumpeters take their parts home to practise them, and where players rave about the Barbican concerts they've just been to. They are full of loyal and friendly music lovers who will give you unstinting support and admiration, not to mention solos and concertos. Think of it as doing your bit to support the arts in your local community, which, of course, it is.

The rules for assisting in amateur orchestras mainly involve avoidance. Avoid getting involved in politicking for or against other hired players. Avoid the urge to correct other players' techniques unless requested. Try to avoid getting dragged into decision-making, unless it's your own prospective concerto that is under discussion, and never agree to play chamber music with anyone whose ability involves any level of guesswork. The range of talent inside the music profession is surprisingly wide; but the range of abilities outside is nothing short of extraordinary: everything from surgeons who could have been soloists to accountants who — bizarre as it seems — can't count for beans.

RULE 35: Chamber music. By all means, have a piano trio, wind quintet etc. Nothing can be more inspiriting than an occasional recital, especially if you have a contact (and you'll probably need one) in one of the few remaining music clubs dotted around the country. Chamber music is almost every performer's dream, and there are still plenty of places to do it as long as you don't expect to get much more than expenses.

You may have to turn down some orchestral work, if there is to be any level of commitment to your ensemble, but with luck the musical rewards will serve as recompense. After all, this is what you went into the rat-race for; this is what enchanted you at music college. As you sit in your grimy ballet pit, opening your fortieth *Nutcracker* of the season, as you blink while the strobe lights of the latest pop singer blast past your stand, as you set your teeth for the latest opera spectacular — remember the time you played Opus 132 while the moonlight spilled in the window. Remember the moment you discovered Schubert. Remember the way you felt performing Ravel's string quartet, the completeness of creating something beautiful.

I look around every orchestra I play in, freelance and full-time, and can spot in a moment the people who have lost what they had when they started. The orchestra member dreaming about her antique china collection who would rather die than put on a classical CD at home; the hard-bitten muso who wishes now he'd read law in the first place; the session player, estranged from the music he once lived for. But for each of these there are others: players who still become excited by a Feuermann recording, seasoned professionals still capable of picking up an instrument at home for the love of it, people who retain the ability to approach life with the freshness we all had before the profession did its best to wrench it away. So don't let the corruption, the greed or the stupidity of the profession grind you down. Be one of the rebels — the rebels of all ages — who defiantly keep hold of their feeling for the music, who still thrill to the sound of trumpets in a Mahler symphony, who make time in their lives to play for love, not only for money. Be one of the many — for we are many — who still care, who still practise, who still dream. Because, as O'Shaughnessy wrote, 'We are the music-makers/And we are the dreamers of dreams.'

The last rule of all is to try to keep hold of the spirit. That's what really makes the struggle worthwhile in the end.

Reviews for Alice McVeigh's
While the Music Lasts and *Ghost Music*

'Characters rise and fall to McVeigh's superbly controlled conductor's baton. The orchestra becomes a universe in microcosm… McVeigh succeeds in harmonising a supremely comic tone with much darker notes.'
The Sunday Times

'McVeigh is a professional cellist and is thus able to describe with wry authority the extraordinary life of a London orchestra. This is a very enjoyable novel, and not quite as light as it pretends to be.'
The Sunday Telegraph

Lisa Jardine, on Radio 3: 'This is an intense and intriguing novel that gives a sense of the throbbing heart of an orchestra.'

'Ever wondered what goes on in the backstage life of a symphony orchestra? This pacy, racy novel was written by one who knows.'
The Daily Mail

David Owen Norris, on Radio 3: 'I found it a gripping read — a kaleidoscope of real characters in real situations. And as for the writing… McVeigh's turn of phrase is positively Wodehousian. She is wonderfully funny.'

'The last night of the Proms will never seem so staid again.'
The Yorkshire Post

'McVeigh is a freelance cellist playing with numerous orchestras, but who would guess that the backstage goings on of an orchestra would provide such a gem of a book?… McVeigh writes amusingly but with authority about the chaotic life of a London orchestra. Even for readers with no interest in music, she entertainingly reveals all aspects of life.'
The Western Morning News